YESHUA KING of EASTER

Written by Jay Risner
Illustrated/Design Layout Jay Risner

Copyright © 2013

ISBN 9780578501598

Library of Congress Control Number: 2019940552

Printed in the United States of America by Ingram Spark/Lightning Source

Published by Spirit Wings Designs 2019
daslpacker55@yahoo.com

Visit at http://mubbus.us/EasterKing/

GOLGOTHA

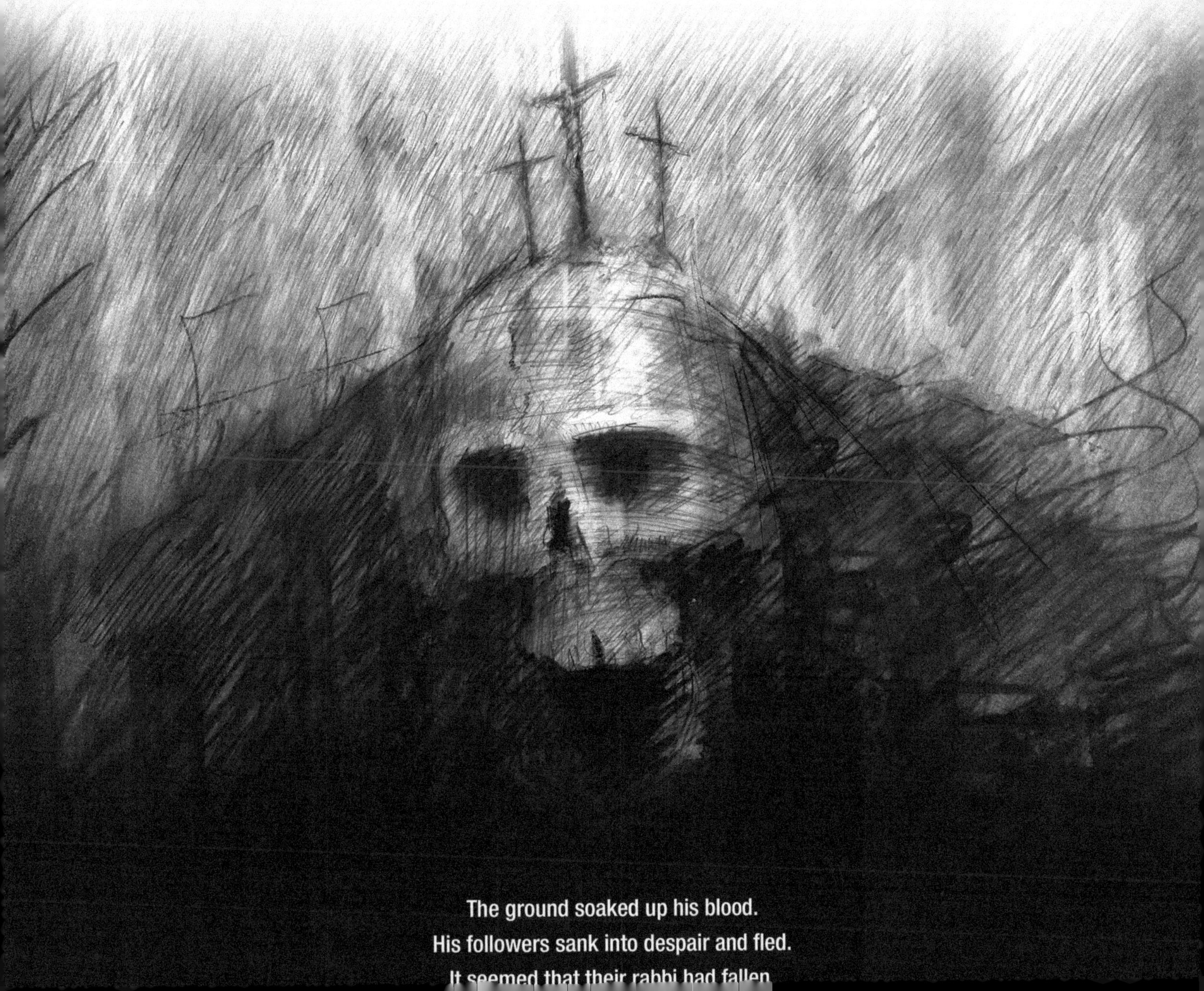

The ground soaked up his blood.

His followers sank into despair and fled.

It seemed that their rabbi had fallen

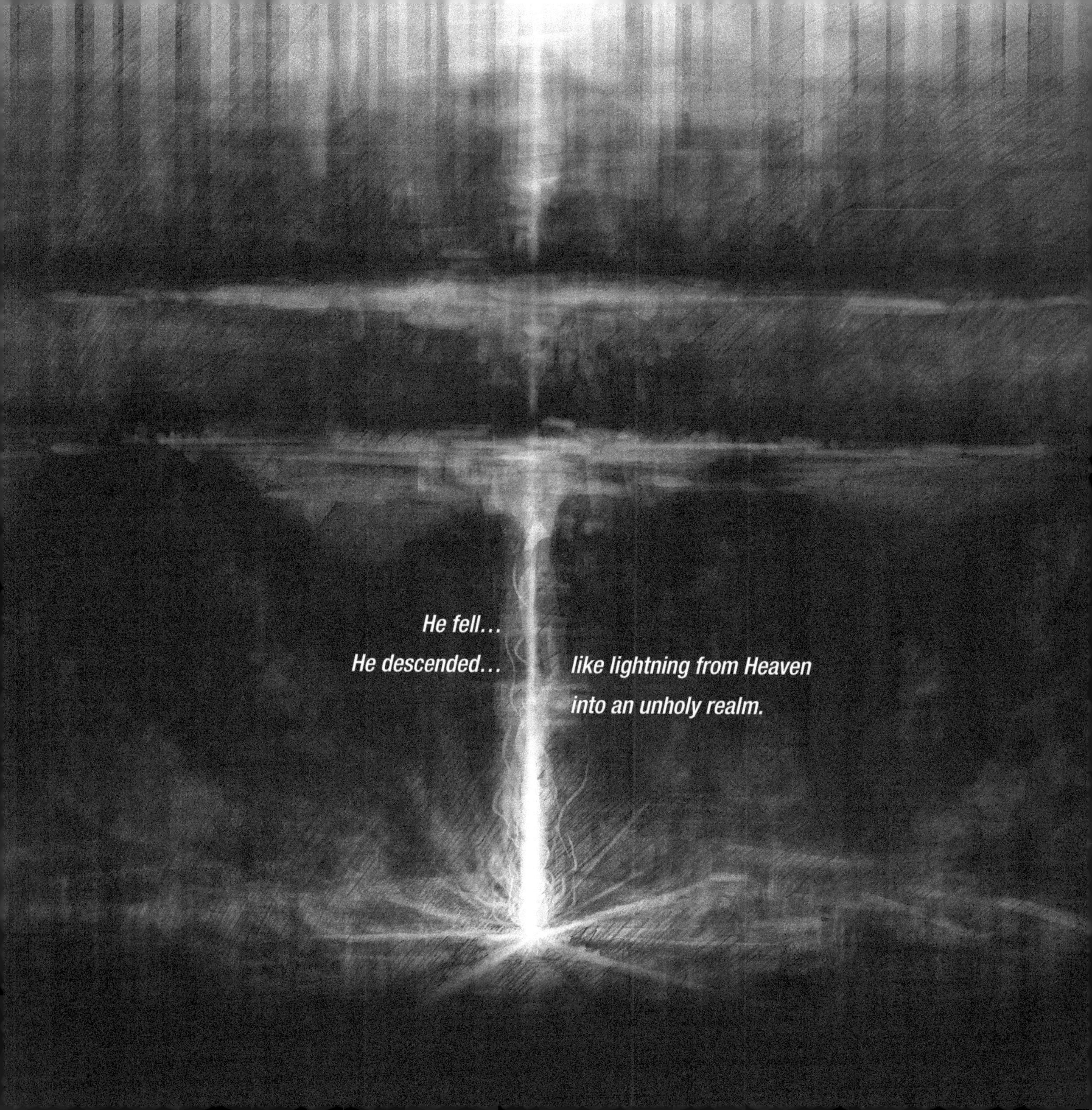

He fell…
He descended…
like lightning from Heaven
into an unholy realm.

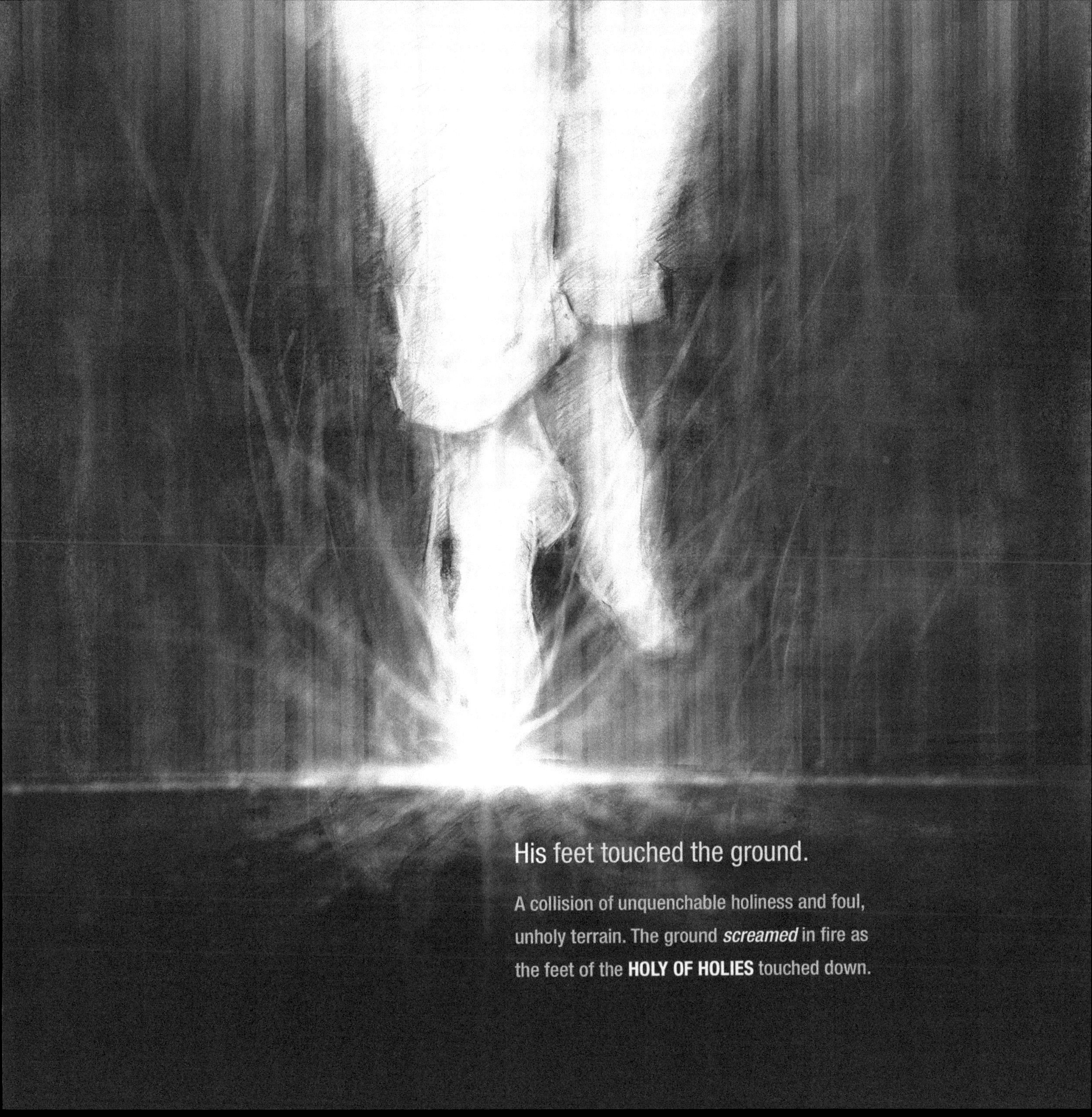

His feet touched the ground.

A collision of unquenchable holiness and foul,
unholy terrain. The ground *screamed* in fire as
the feet of the **HOLY OF HOLIES** touched down.

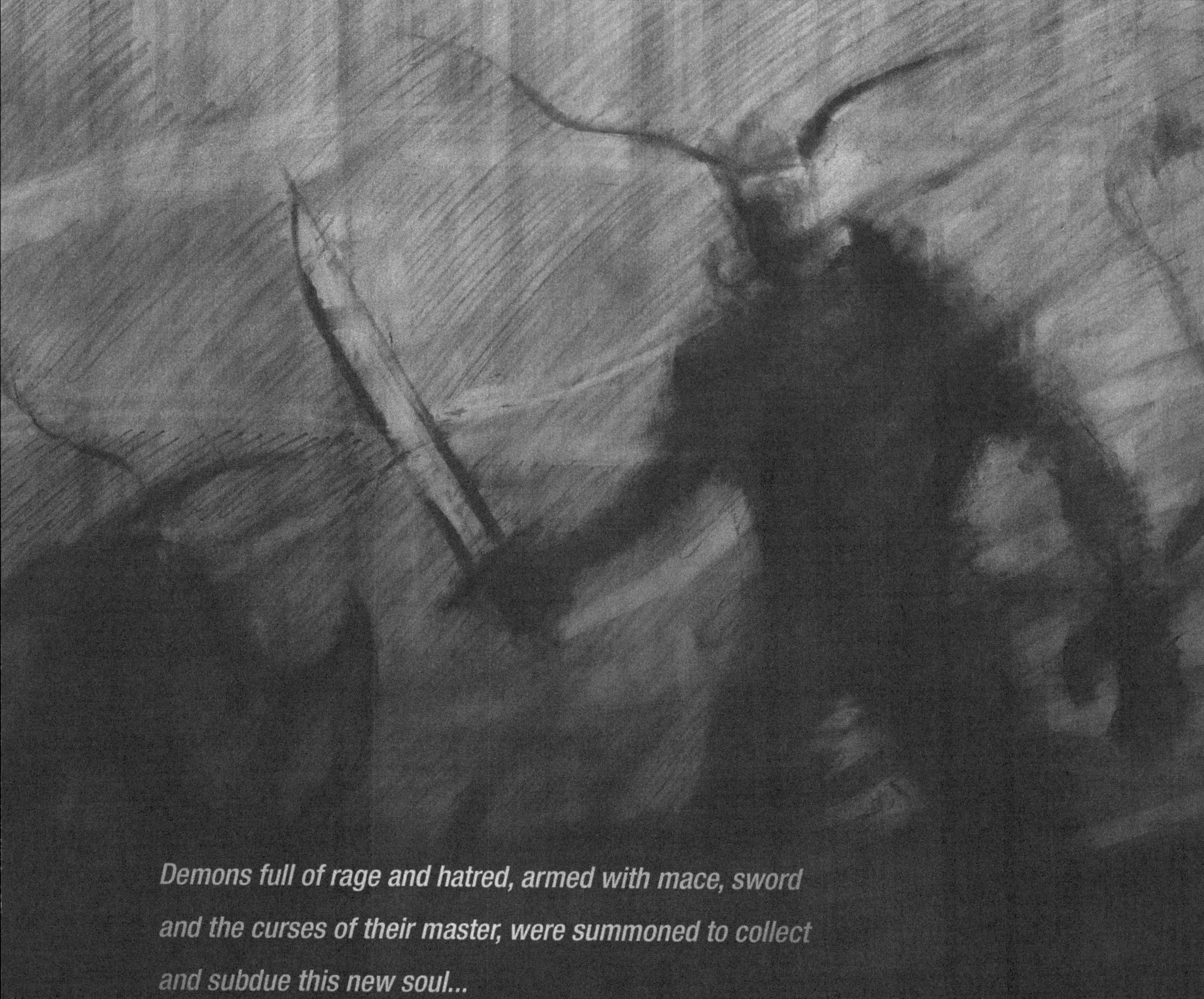
Demons full of rage and hatred, armed with mace, sword
and the curses of their master, were summoned to collect
and subdue this new soul...

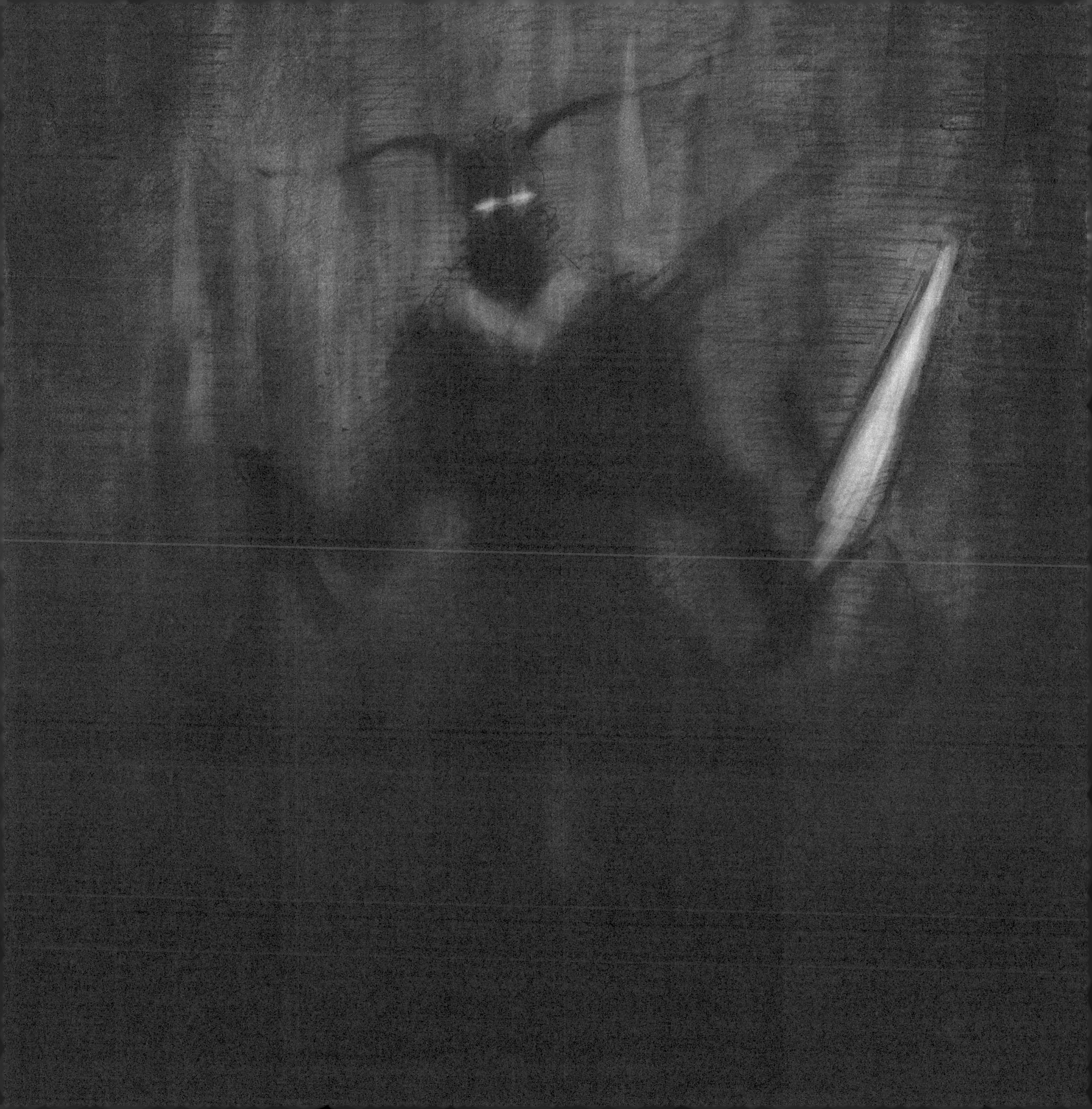

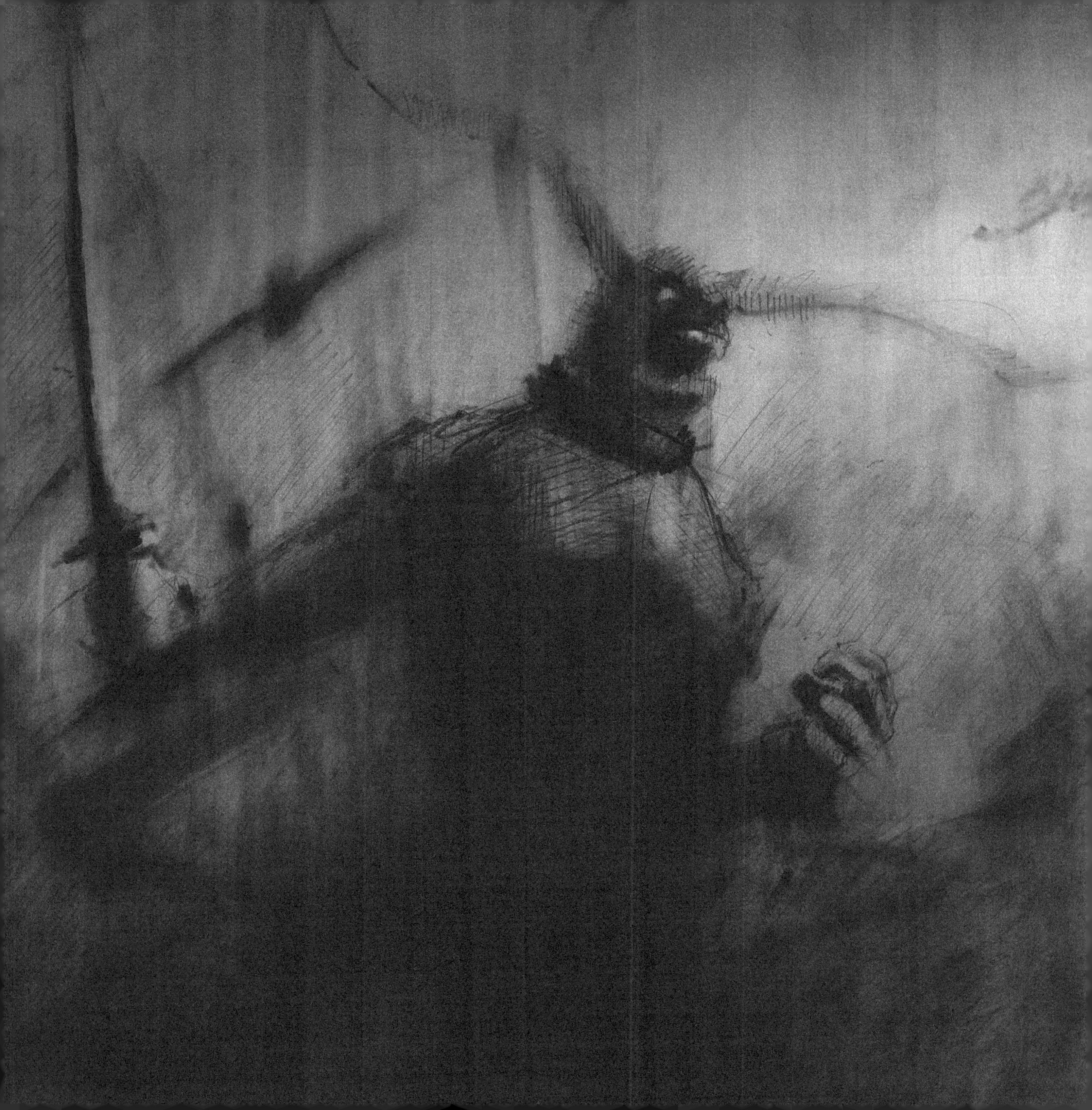

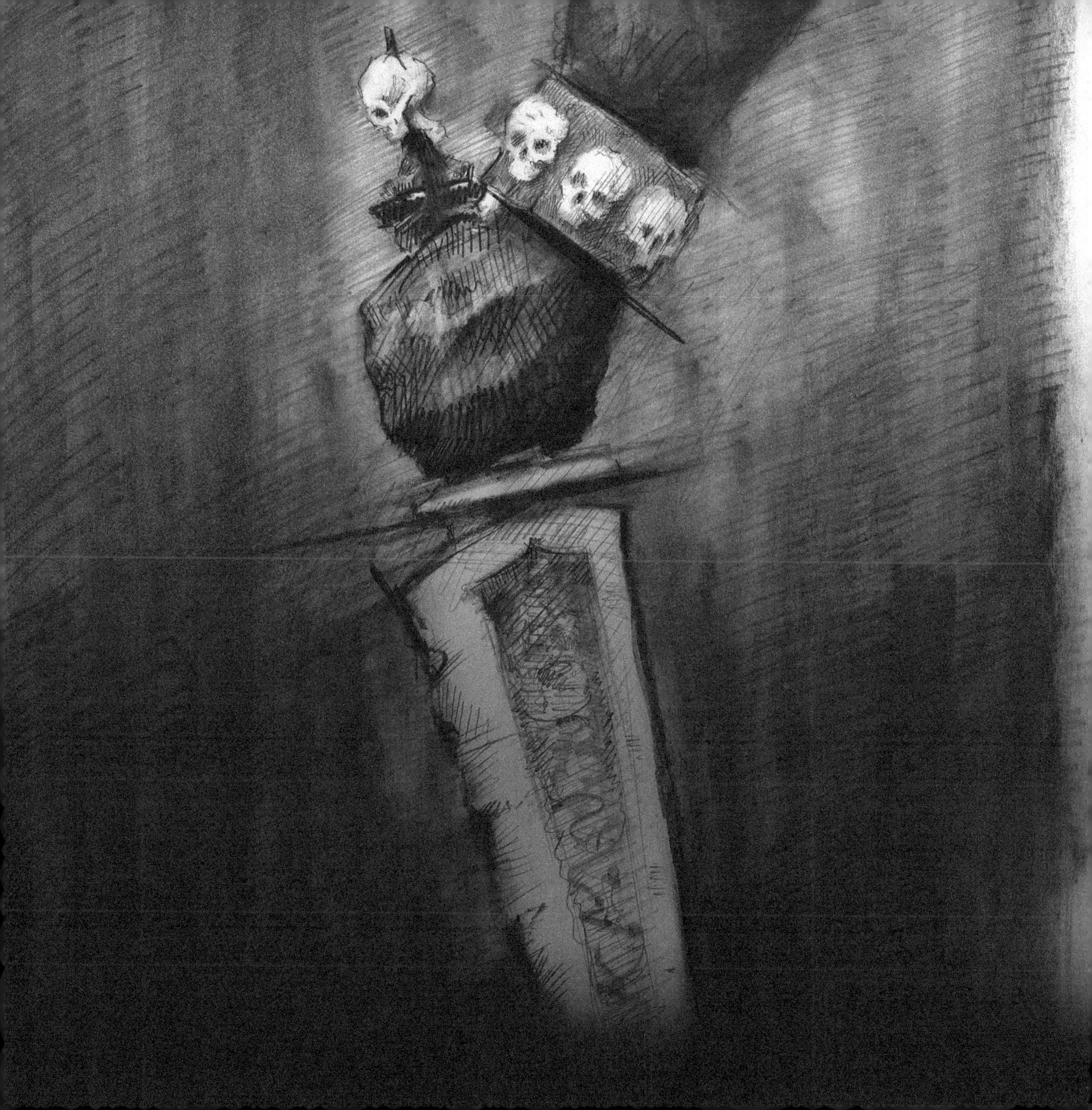

....they failed.

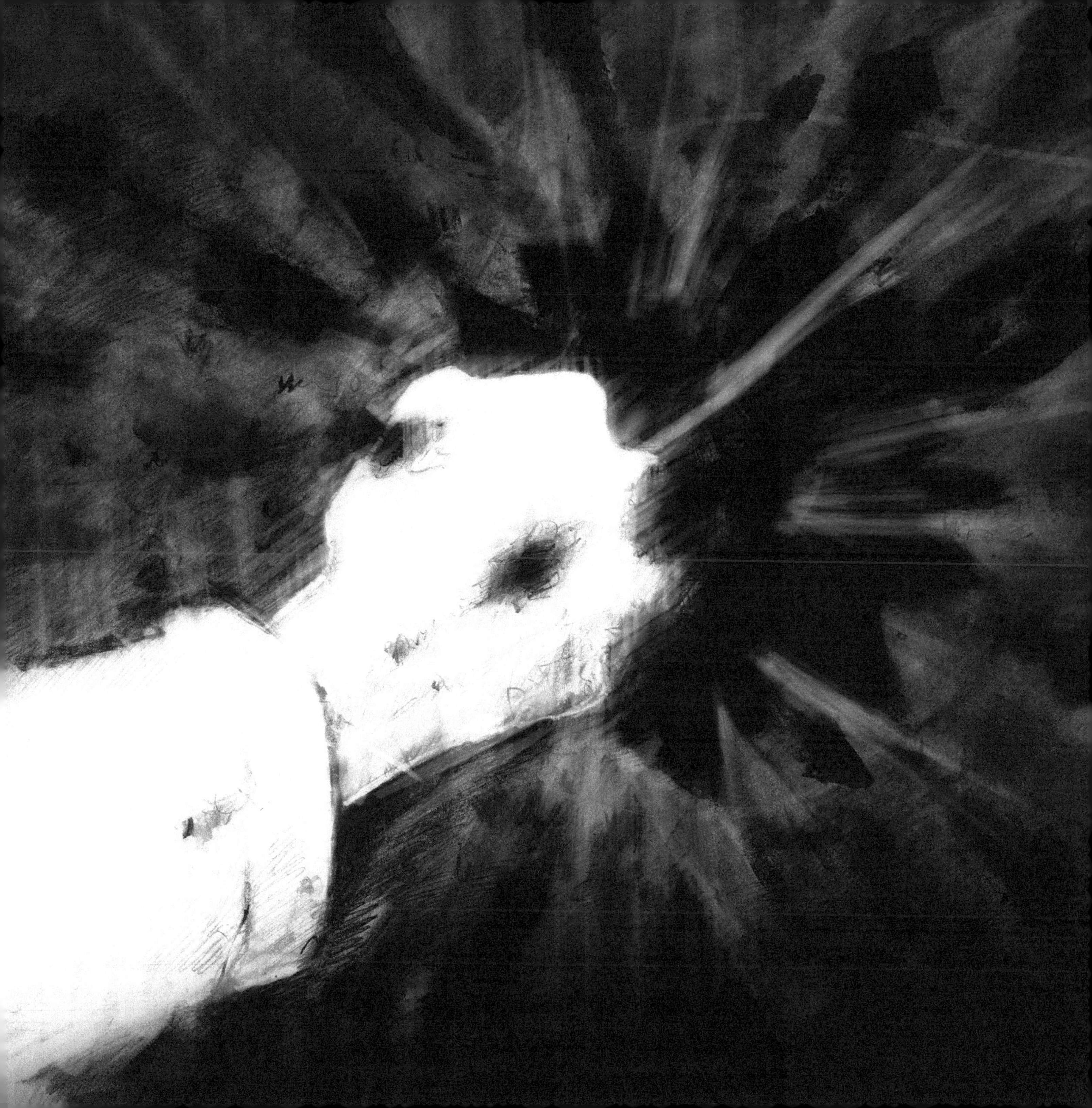

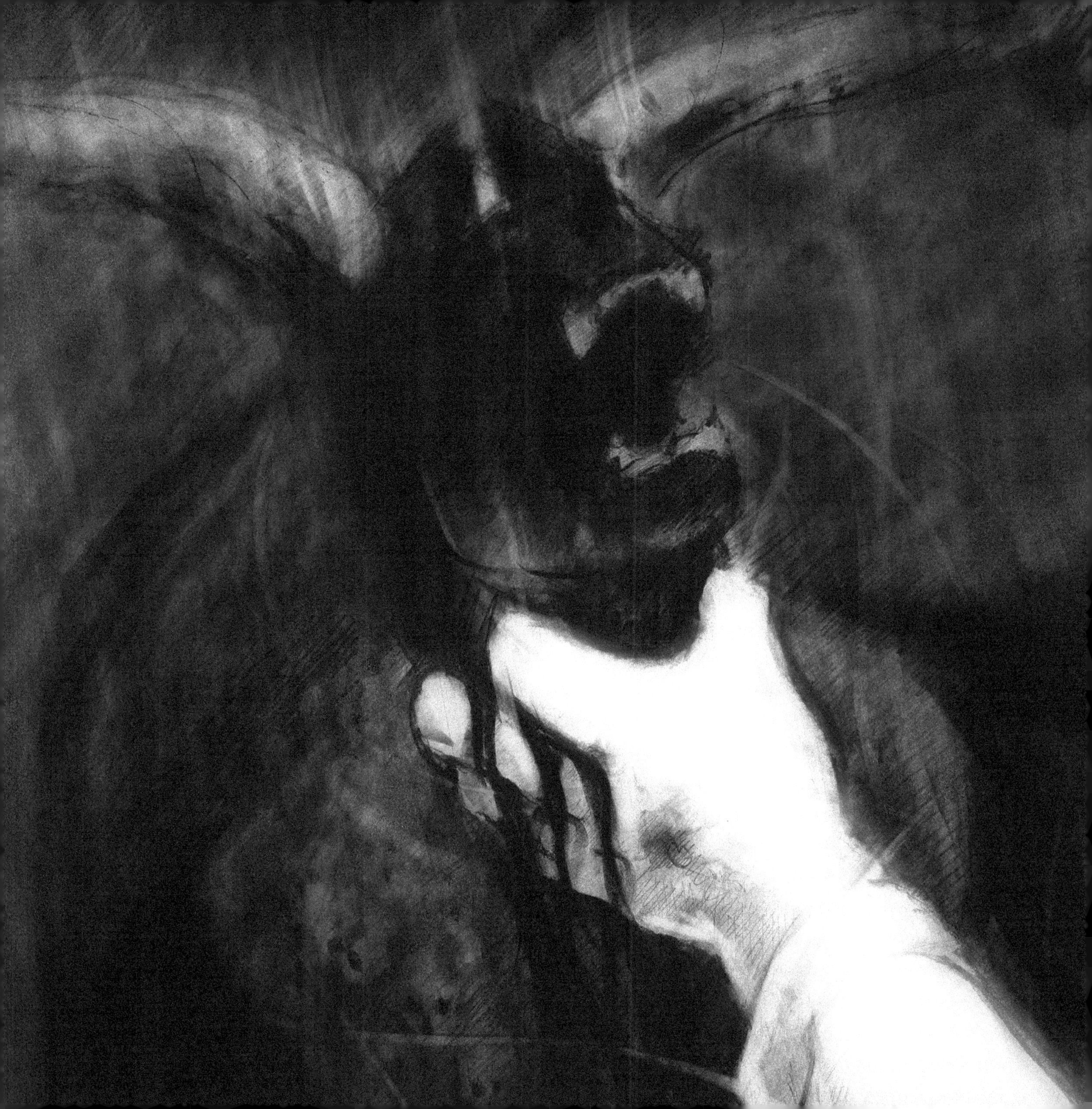

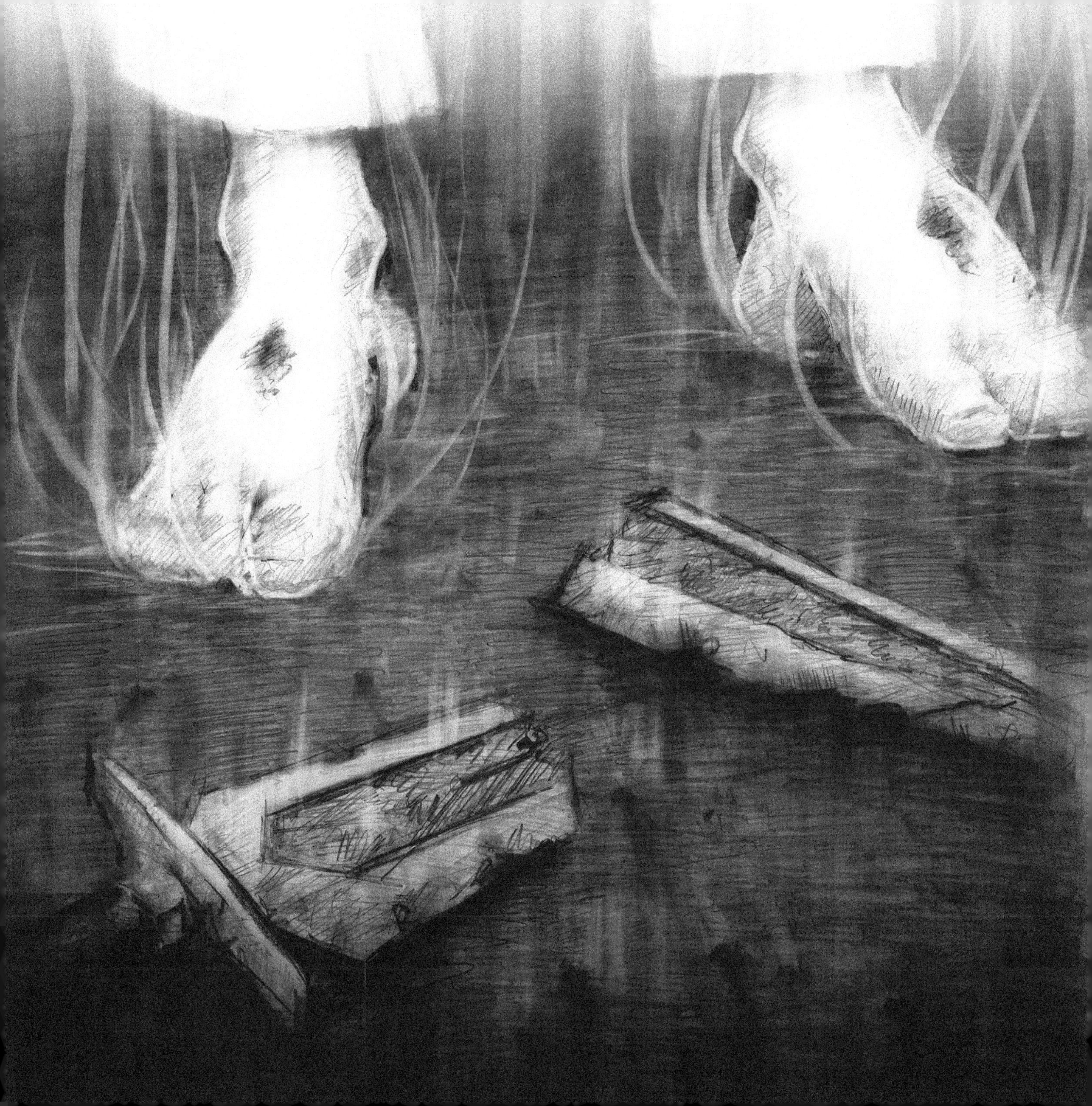

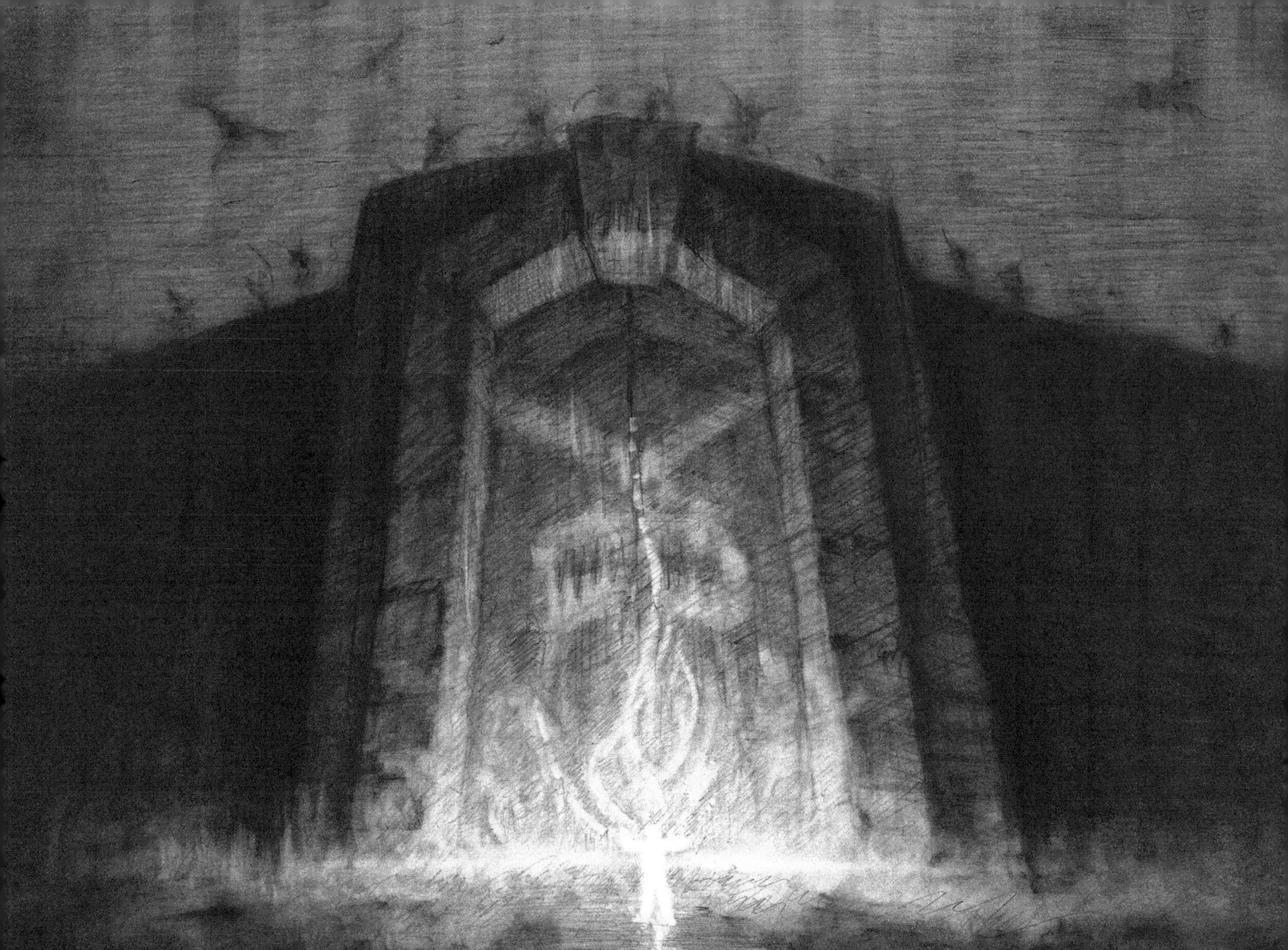

The **HOLY INVADER,**
truly an army of one, advances.

The ground itself smolders under the blazing footsteps,
and he approaches the gates of the stronghold of the enemy.

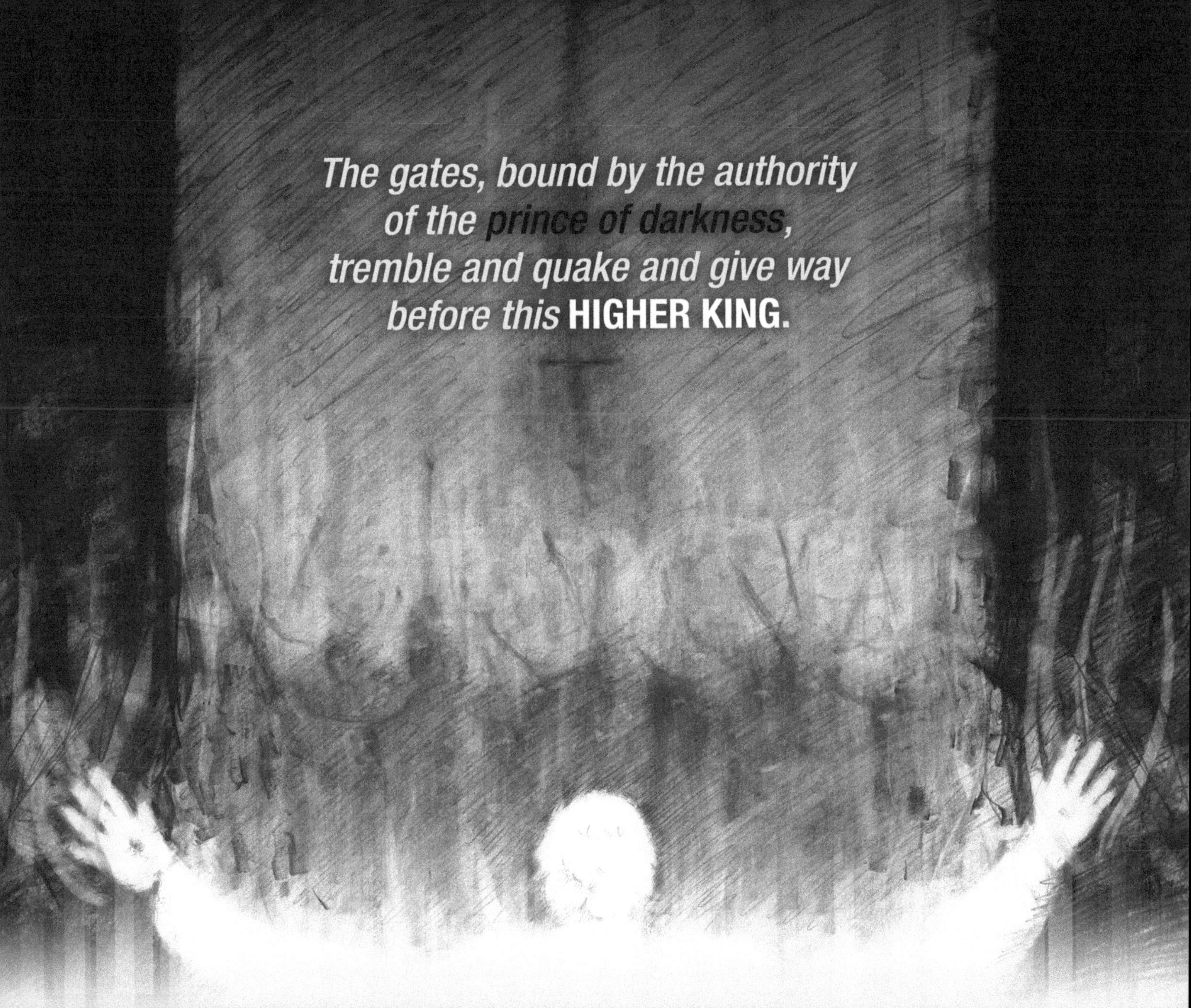

The gates, bound by the authority
of the prince of darkness,
tremble and quake and give way
before this HIGHER KING.

To utter HIS name is to give praise to God. His name is a thousand names:
**Yeshua, King, King of Kings, Lord of Lords, Alpha, Omega, King Eternal,
King of Righteousness, Lion of Judah, The Rock, The Great I Am,
The Truth, The Captain of Salvation, The Judge, The Holy One of God,
The Holy King of Israel, The Holy King of All Creation,**

HOLY   HOLY   HOLY.

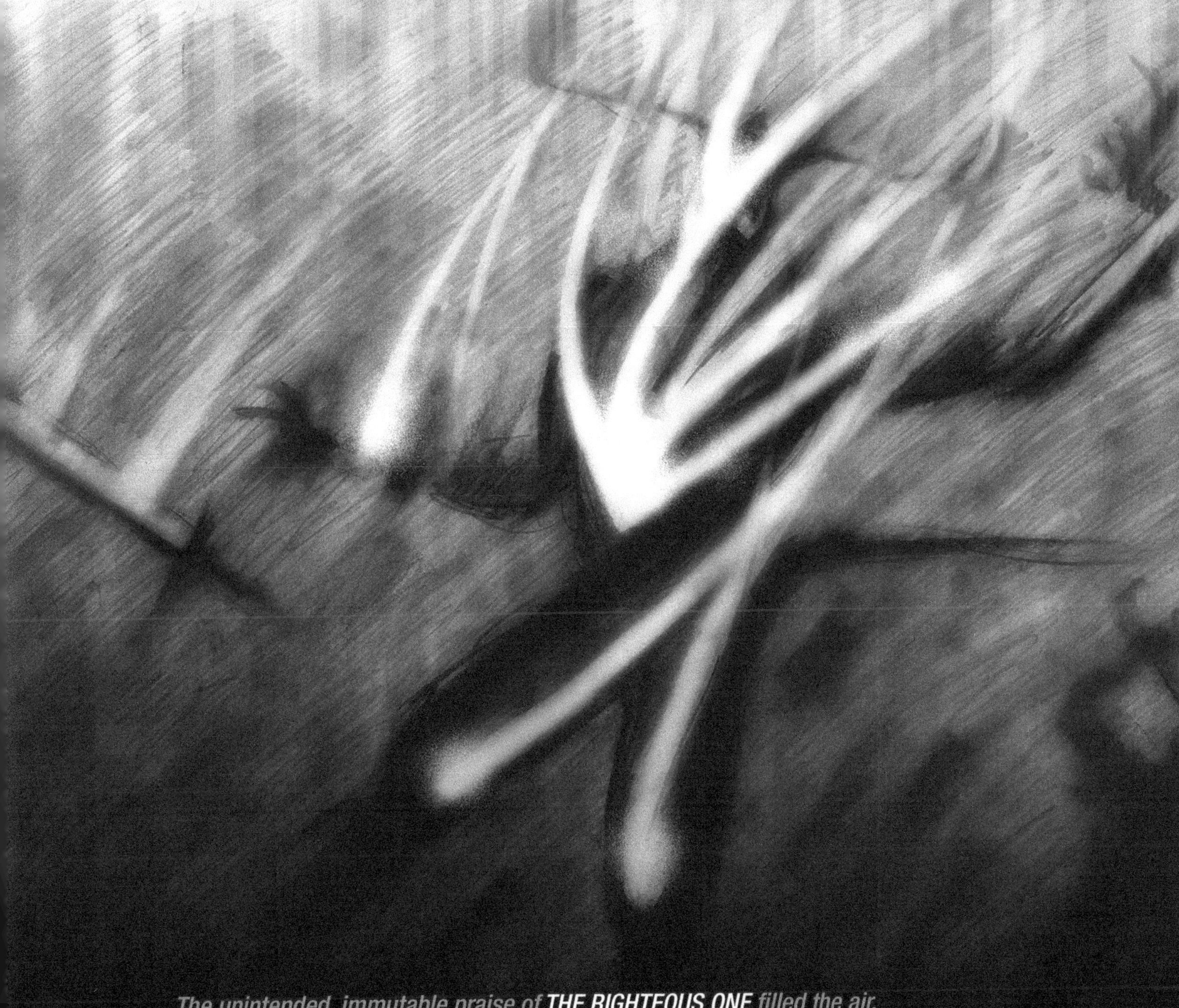

The unintended, immutable praise of **THE RIGHTEOUS ONE** filled the air.
To utter **HIS** name is to give praise to God, and the demon was consumed by holy fire.

*When you see **HIM** you see the FATHER…*
and there **HE** is right before them.

*Destruction, the fire of God, the Judgement of God, the Hammer of God's Wrath
had fallen on them this night and they fled!*

*And then... the mouth that spoke at the beginning of time and uttered words that gave birth to the
Universe: atoms and stars... time itself... opened.*

HE SPOKE...

*It was an **explosion** of lightning – a simple rebuke from the mouth of God.*

*A thousand demons were consumed by fire,
ten thousand fell, a million more fled in terror.*

The fire went all the way to the throne of the cursed prince of darkness himself.

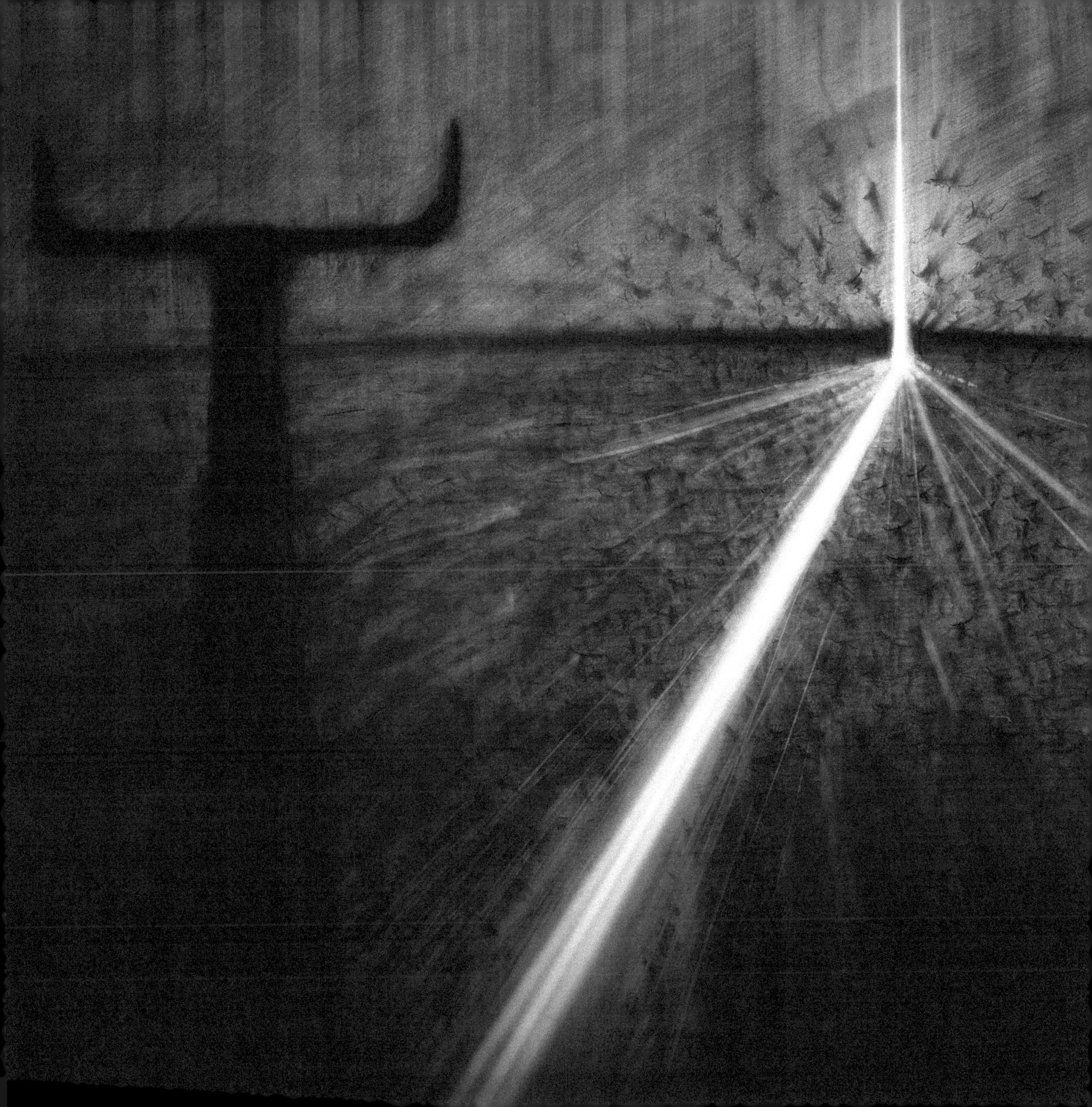

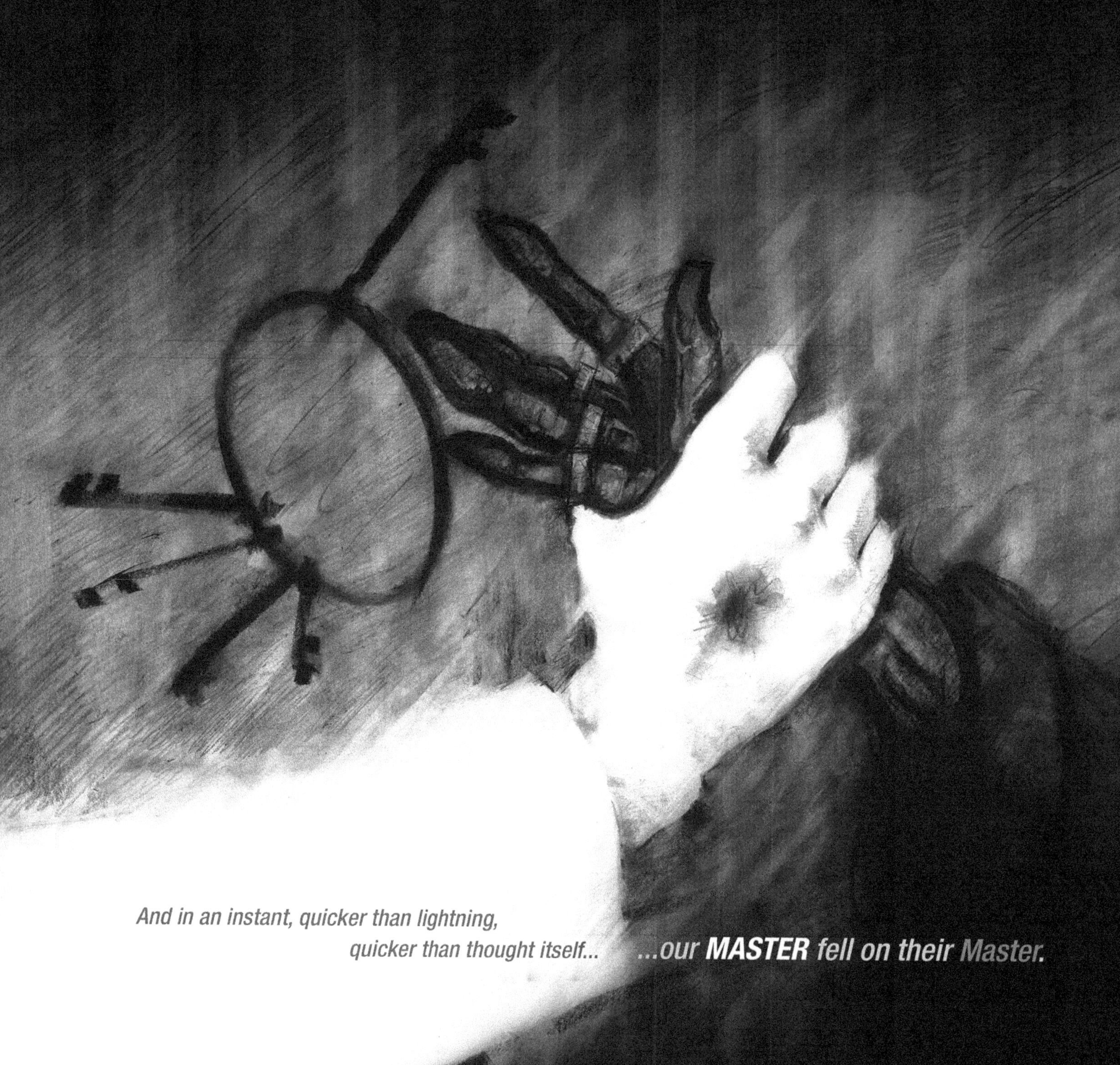

And in an instant, quicker than lightning,
quicker than thought itself...   ...our MASTER fell on their Master.

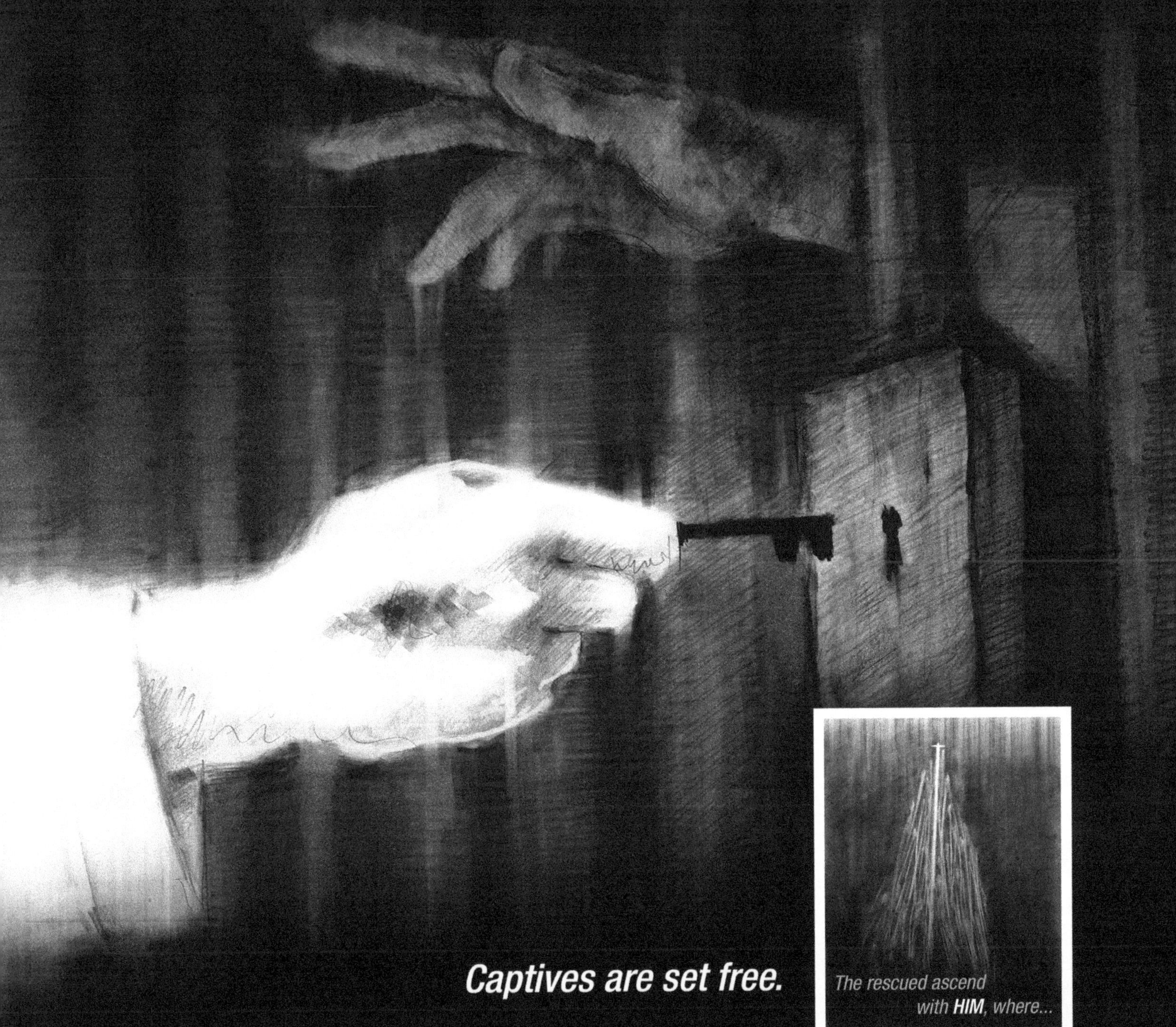
Captives are set free.
The rescued ascend
with HIM, where...

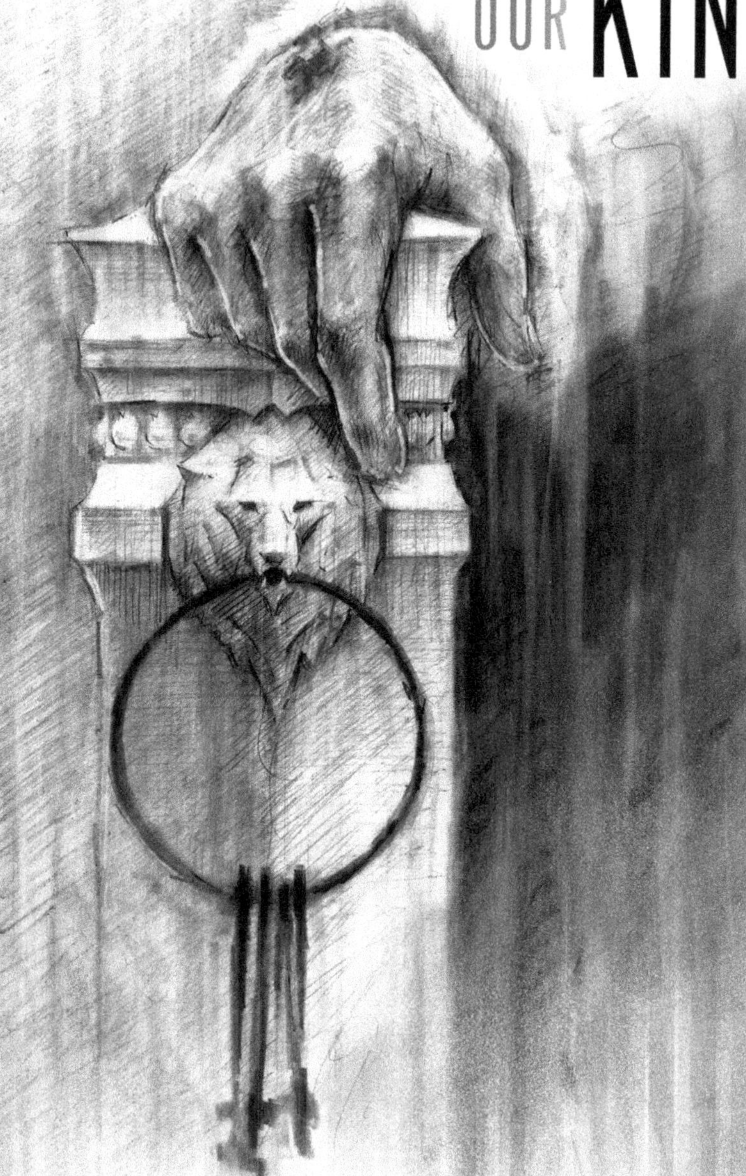HE reigns... seated on HIS throne
OUR KING
Forever and ever and ever...   AMEN